Level 7

MASTERWORK CLASSICS
COMPILED AND EDITED BY JANE MAGRATH

CONTENTS

Cover art: Planet Art

FOREWORD

THE MUSIC

Compositions in *Masterwork Classics* have been chosen first for the quality of the music, since it is the heart of a student's study. Great care has been given to choosing music that is of substance so that the student can quickly discover the character, spirit and temperament of each composition. Some pieces are familiar favorites while others, although seldom heard, are sure to become favorites with students and teachers alike. Recital and contest groupings can be put together with ease from these volumes.

Students playing the music in *Masterwork Classics* will have been exposed to a significant range of pieces from the standard classical teaching literature. They will have studied representative selections from the most significant works written by the standard composers through the centuries, including the Bach *Short Preludes* and *Inventions,* Schumann *Album for the Young,* Mendelssohn *Songs without Words,* miscellaneous compositions of Chopin, compositions from the Russian pedagogical schools including works by Maykapar and Bortkievich; and others by Bartók and Debussy.

THE LEVELING

A great deal of care has been given to providing literature that progresses smoothly from level to level in these volumes. Some students will play many or most of the compositions in a book from *Masterwork Classics,* while others will play less, moving more rapidly as they progress to the advanced standard literature.

EDITORIAL PRINCIPLES

All literature in this book is based on the earliest possible editions. Fingerings have been added, and teachers and students should alter fingerings to fit the performer's hand as needed. Articulation markings and sparse dynamic markings have been added in a few situations, primarily in works from the Baroque period. Pedaling decisions should be undertaken with the utmost care, and such markings generally are not added editorially since pedaling will vary from piano to piano and from hall to hall due to acoustical considerations.

SUGGESTED ORDER OF STUDY

This order of study is suggested only. Teachers should feel free to use an alternative progression for their special pedagogical purposes.

Concepts listed below are musical/technical considerations in working out a piece.

Short Prelude in C Major

BWV 933

Johann Sebastian Bach
(1685–1750)

Short Prelude in D Minor
BWV 935

Johann Sebastian Bach
(1685–1750)

Invention in F Major
BWV 779

Johann Sebastian Bach
(1685–1750)

Sonatina in A Minor

Georg Anton Benda
(1722–1795)

Sonatina in G Major
Op. 55, No. 2 (first movement)

Friedrich Kuhlau
(1786–1832)

(b) Play the small note very quickly, on the beat.

Sonatina in C Major
Op. 55, No. 3 (first movement)

Friedrich Kuhlau
(1786–1832)

Allegro con spirito

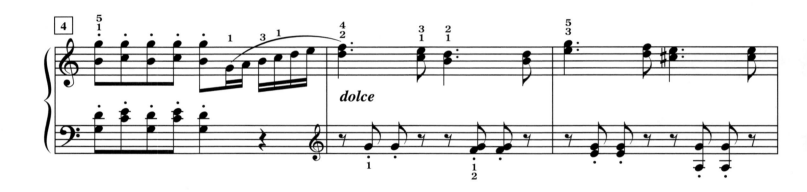

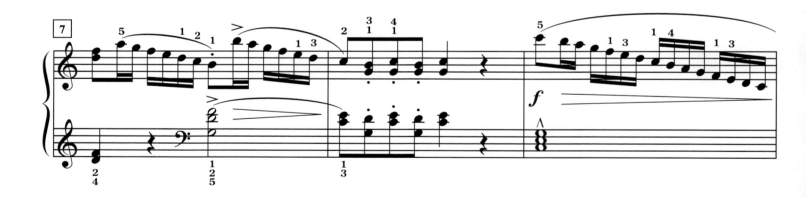

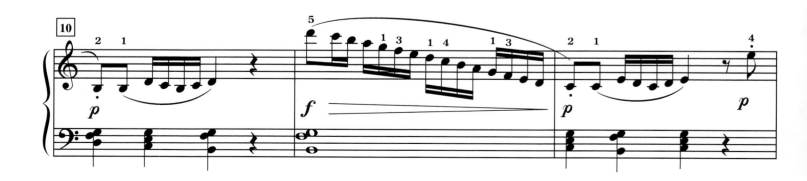

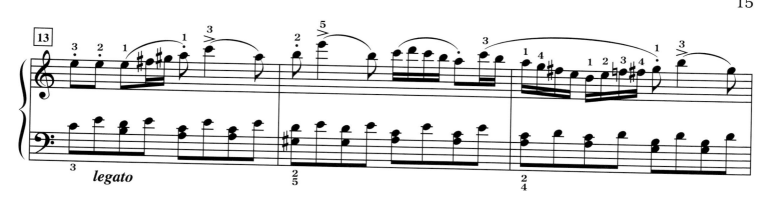

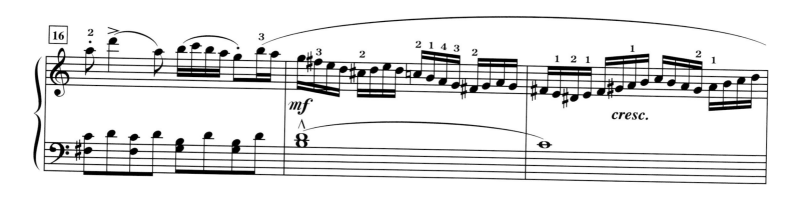

Für Elise
WoO 59

Ludwig van Beethoven
(1770–1827)

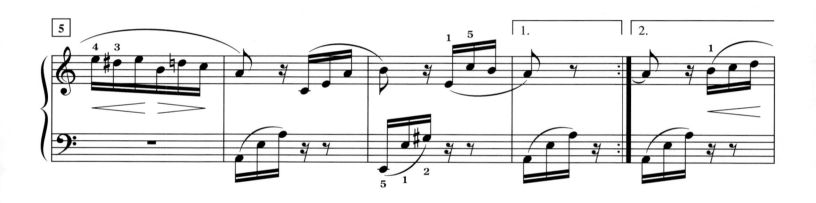

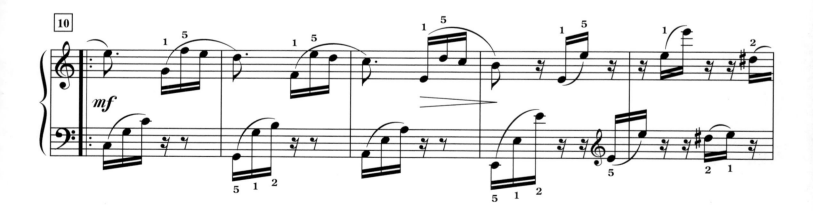

Valse in A-flat Major

D. 365 (Op. 9a), No. 12

Franz Schubert
(1797–1828)

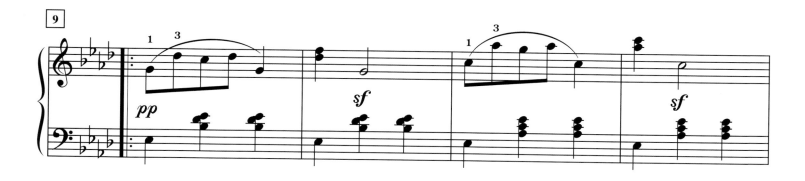

Valse Noble in A Minor

D. 969 (Op. 77), No. 9

Franz Schubert
(1797–1828)

Album Leaf

Opus Posthumous

Frédéric Chopin
(1810–1849)

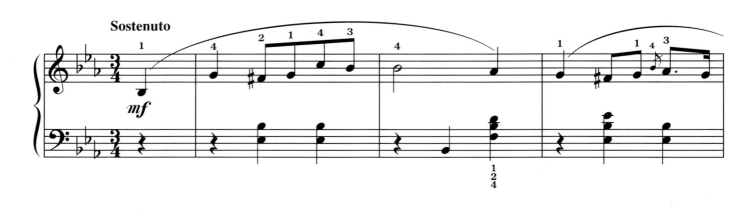

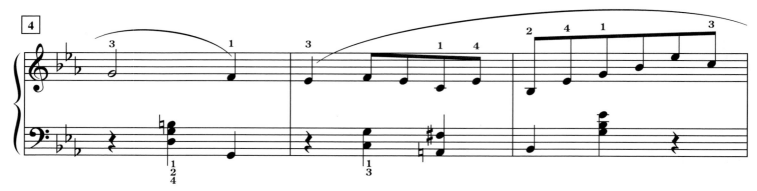

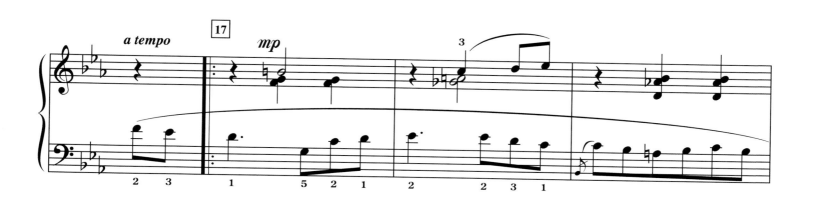

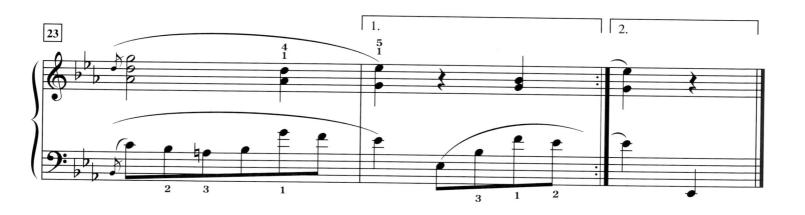

Prelude in E Minor

Op. 28, No. 4

Frédéric Chopin
(1810–1849)

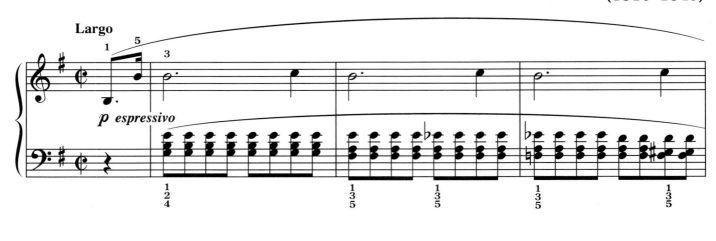

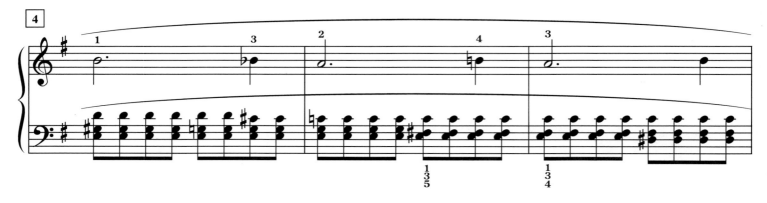

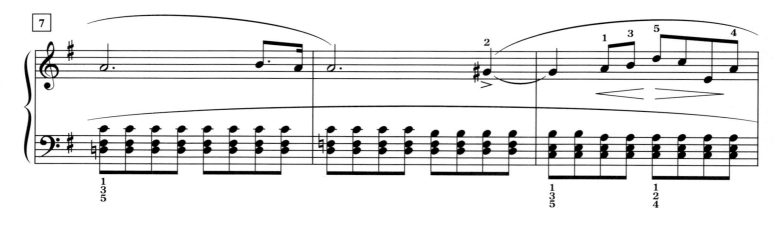

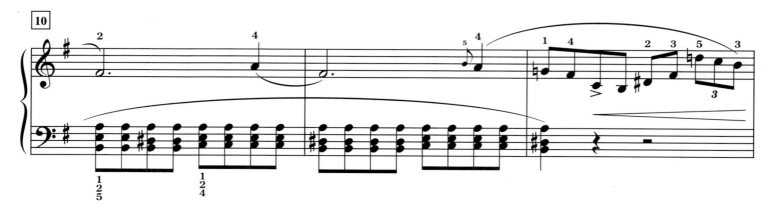

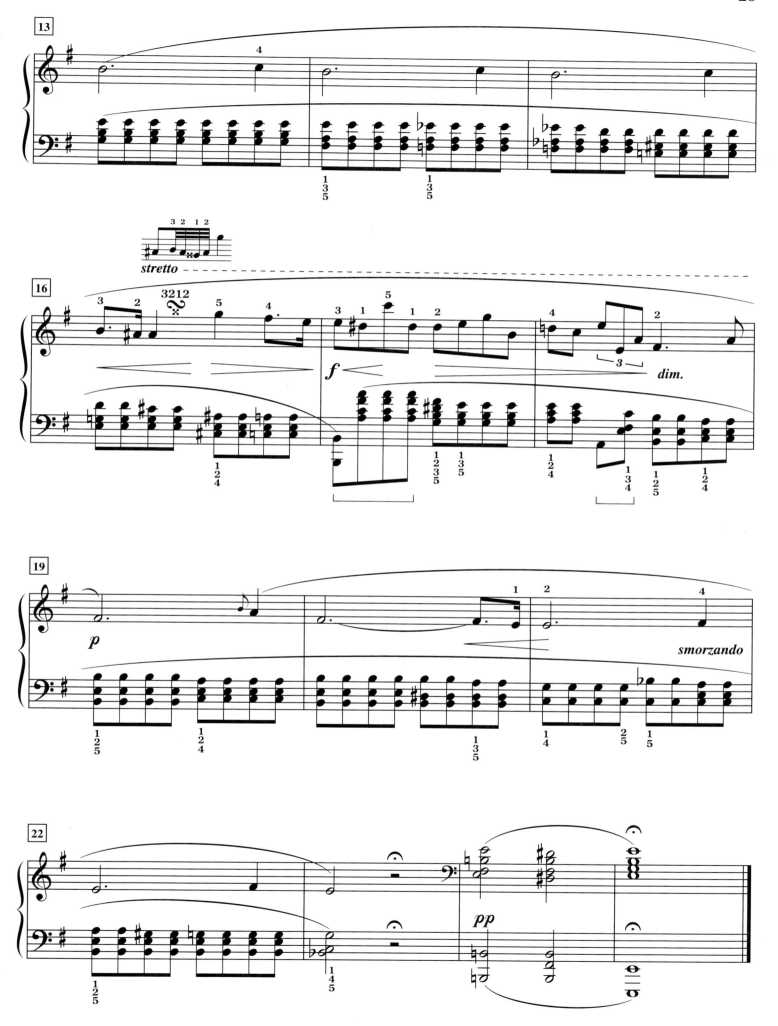

Waltz in A Minor
Opus Posthumous

Frédéric Chopin
(1810–1849)

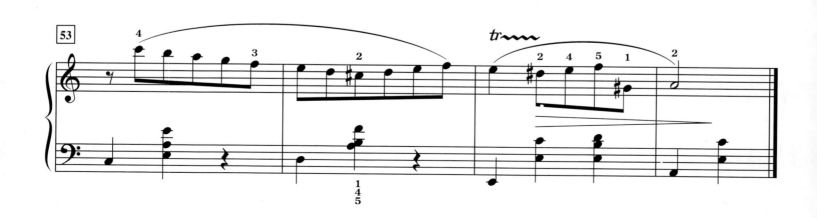

Knight Rupert
Op. 68, No. 12

Robert Schumann
(1810–1856)

(a) Blustering, unyielding

The Horseman
Op. 68, No. 23

Robert Schumann
(1810–1856)

ⓐ Short and precise

ⓑ Nach und nach schwächer

ⓑ Gradually softer

The Little Girls' Dance
Op. 36, No. 3

Niels Gade
(1817–1890)

Fluttering Leaves in A Minor
Op. 147, No. 2

Carl Kölling
(1831–1914)

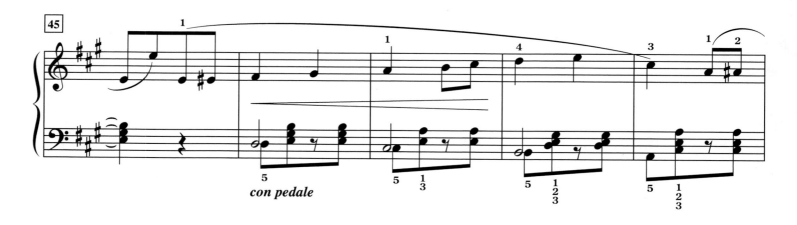

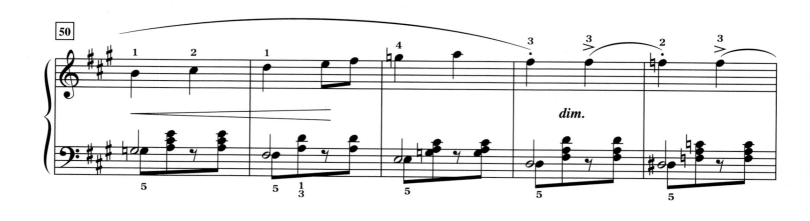

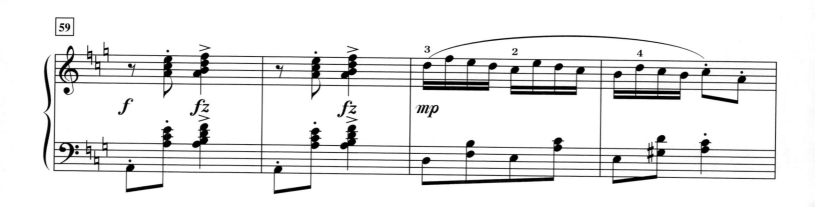

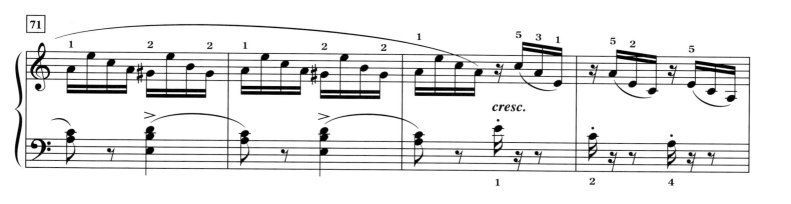

Song without Words

(Consolation)
Op. 30, No. 3

Felix Mendelssohn
(1809–1847)

Adagio non troppo

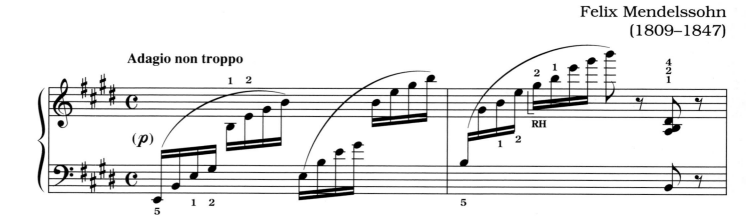

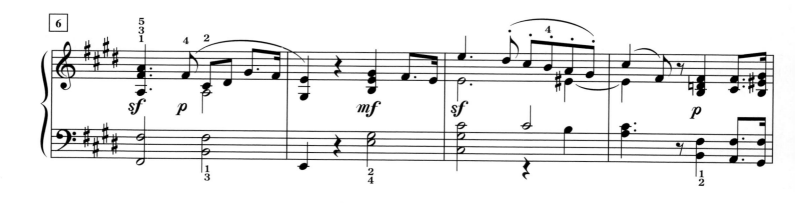